CHESHIRE
MOODS

ALAN NOVELLI

HALSGROVE

First published in Great Britain in 2007

Title page photograph: *Evening light illuminates the eighteenth-century folly of Mow Cop Castle on the Cheshire / Staffordshire border.*

British Library Cataloguing-in-Publication Data
A CIP record for this title is available from the British Library

ISBN 978 1 84114 608 9

HALSGROVE
Halsgrove House, Ryelands Farm Industrial Estate,
Bagley Green, Wellington, Somerset TA21 9PZ
Tel: 01823 653777 Fax: 01823 216796
email: sales@halsgrove.com
website: www.halsgrove.com

Printed and bound by D'Auria Industrie Grafiche, Italy

*To Gaby my beautiful wife,
thank you for your support and for tolerating my photographic obsession.
And for Mum and Dad, thanks for everything.*

Introduction

Cheshire is one of England's best-kept secrets. This 'teapot' shaped county of beauty and character, combines both scenic splendour and topographical diversity to produce an utterly awe-inspiring landscape.

The rugged, sometimes harsh nature of Cheshire's own slice of the Peak District National Park offers a heady mix of both solitude and serenity. These features provide the catalyst for arguably, some of the most delightful walking scenery to be discovered anywhere in the northwest of England.

However, the rolling peaks make up only a small part of this magnificent county and Cheshire often remains characterised by the wide expanse of its renowned Plain. It is here that the black and white façades of Cheshire's elaborate half-timbered and so-called 'Magpie' buildings compete for attention in a landscape punctuated by tall escarpments, undulating hills and chocolate-box scenes. Landmarks such as the mighty Jodrell Bank Radio Telescope and twin castles of Beeston and Peckforton rise dramatically from the countryside offering astounding views of man's influence upon the landscape.

Historically too, the county is rich in heritage. The Romans mined salt from the central 'Wich' or 'Salt' towns, building the fortress of Deva at Chester to protect their operations. Later the Norman Earls hunted in the vast royal forests of Delamere and Macclesfield, before these same forests provided the timbers used to construct many of the county's Magpie buildings. Later still, a network of canals and rivers were utilised to criss-cross the Cheshire landscape demonstrating the county's prominence for silk and cotton manufacture during the Industrial Revolution. It is these same rivers, canals and meres (or lakes) that now feature prominently in the landscape and are included within many of the scenes within *Cheshire Moods*.

Ultimately though it is light that helps to create the atmospheric images contained within these pages. It is no accident that many of the images in this book were taken during the first and last hour of the day, for it is precisely these conditions that allow the golden rays of low raking sunlight to show the landscape at its very finest.

Cheshire Moods is the result of one photographer's ambition, which was to produce a book showcasing Cheshire at its very best. Images from all four seasons, taken at every conceivable time of the day are included within these pages and my hope is that you will enjoy seeing them as much as I have enjoyed producing them.

Alan Novelli

MAP OF CHESHIRE

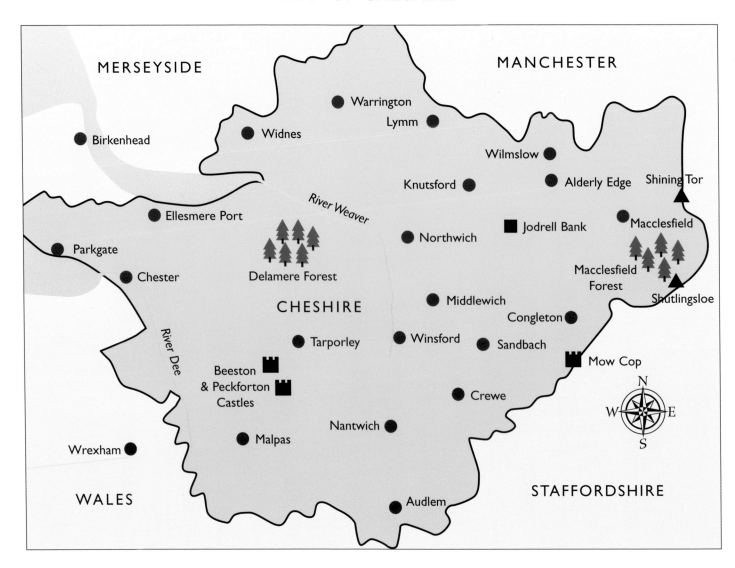

MERSEYSIDE

MANCHESTER

Warrington

Lymm

Birkenhead

Widnes

Wilmslow

Knutsford

Alderly Edge

Shining Tor

Ellesmere Port

River Weaver

Jodrell Bank

Macclesfield

Parkgate

Northwich

Chester

Delamere Forest

Macclesfield
Forest

CHESHIRE

Shutlingsloe

River Dee

Middlewich

Congleton

Tarporley

Winsford

Sandbach

Beeston
& Peckforton
Castles

Mow Cop

Crewe

N

W   E

S

Nantwich

Wrexham

Malpas

WALES

Audlem

STAFFORDSHIRE

'The Rows' at Night from the City Walls, Eastgate Street, Chester
The black and white timber-framed buildings of 'The Rows' are one of Chester's
most iconic symbols. Dating from medieval times, they are shown here whilst
twilight still paints the sky. The long camera exposure has allowed the lights of
moving vehicles to record as streaks and the movement of clouds to be shown
as an atmospheric ethereal effect.

Chester Cathedral and the City Walls in Winter
The city walls of Chester are unique in Britain as they allow visitors to completely circumnavigate the ancient defensive ramparts.   They are also perhaps the best way to tour the city, as many of Chester's historic structures can easily be viewed from them. Here, glorious winter sunlight bathes the walls of Chester's grandest building, the Grade 1 Listed Cathedral of Christ and the Blessed Virgin Mary.

Red Fishing Boat on the River Dee below Grosvenor Bridge, Chester
The Listed Grade 1 Grosvenor Bridge was constructed to span the River Dee in the late 1820s.
Sandstone quarried from the Peckforton Hills was used to create this magnificent structure, which has a
single segmental arch of 200 feet. At the time it was the largest single-span stone-arch bridge in Europe.

Roman Legionnaires in Chester's Roman Gardens
Chester was one of three flagship Roman fortresses in Britain. Established in AD43, it was known then as DEVA and housed between 4 and 6 thousand men. Today, stone artefacts from Roman structures can be seen at close quarters in the gardens and tours hosted by Roman Legionnaires can often be spotted offering a truly authentic experience.

The Victorian Eastgate Clock at Night, City Walls, Chester
The Eastgate Clock is perhaps the best known of Chester's sights and was erected to
commemorate Queen Victoria's Diamond Jubilee in 1897. This exquisite timepiece
sits astride the ancient walls, guarding the eastern entrance to the city centre.

Elephants at Chester Zoo
Widely regarded as one of Europe's best zoos and certainly the largest zoo in the United Kingdom,
Chester Zoological Gardens feature over 5000 animals within an 80-acre setting of award winning gardens.
Popular attractions include the Elephants, Black Rhinos and Jaguars – but there is almost every conceivable animal here.

Gibbet Windmill in Summer, near Great Saughall
Gibbet Windmill dates from 1773 and is the last remaining sailed windmill in Cheshire.
Its sails are not all that they seem though. They are actually scaled down, three-quarter sized
copies of the originals, having been replaced when the mill became a private residence.

Sunset over the Dee Estuary, near Parkgate
This spectacular sunset was taken over the tidal sands of the Dee Estuary. Seabirds can be seen on the far sandbanks where a plentiful supply of food will be left by the ebbing tide.

The Seafront at Parkgate on the Wirral
In the early eighteenth century, Parkgate was a prominent seafaring port until the Dee Estuary
silted up and the sands became overgrown with sea grasses. Nowadays it is popular with birdwatchers
and tourists who come to enjoy the delights of its black and white seafront promenade.

The Ellesmere Port Boat Museum
The world's largest floating collection of inland waterways craft is found here within a 7-acre
museum site at the Ellesmere Port Boat Museum. Heritage aplenty can be discovered here,
from old narrowboats, barges and pleasure craft to Dockers cottages, old engines and pump houses.

'The Pit' and Dixon Cottages in Late Summer
The village pond at Christleton is actually an old marl pit dating from the fifteenth century.
The marl, a type of limy clay, was then used to make bricks for the construction of Christleton's early buildings.
In this image we see the beautiful black and white Dixon Cottages reflected in 'The Pit,' whilst the onset
of autumn can be just detected in the colouration of the surrounding trees.

Road Sign in Aldford, near Chester
The charming estate village of Aldford has grown up under the careful nurturing
of the Grosvenor family seated at the nearby Eaton Estate and home to the Duke
of Westminster. One charming feature of the village is its red and white road
signs, which bear the golden symbol of a Talbot Hunting Dog (now extinct).
This emblem forms part of the Grosvenor family's Coat of Arms.

The Cast Iron Bridge and River Dee, near Aldford
A calm and frosty morning shows off the cast iron bridge leading to the Duke of
Westminster's Eaton Estate near the village of Aldford south of Chester.

Farndon Bridge and the River Dee
This medieval sandstone bridge dates from 1345 and spans the River Dee marking the English and Welsh border between the towns of Farndon and Holt. The bridge is said to be haunted by the ghosts of two children whose cries can be heard echoing beneath the bridge in the dead of a stormy night.

Springtime at St Oswald's Parish Church in Malpas
Originally a site of Anglo-Saxon worship, the present magnificent sandstone church of St Oswald's was constructed in the latter half of the fourteenth century. It has two chapels, one commemorating the Brereton family and the other the Cholmondeley family. Both families have featured prominently in the history of Malpas.

Evening Light Illuminates St Michael's Church at Marbury
Boasting perhaps the finest setting of any church in the county, St Michael's at Marbury sits upon a grassy knoll overlooking the waters of 'Big Mere' in south Cheshire. Here we see the final golden rays of evening sunlight lighting the western façade of the church tower, casting a shimmering reflection in the still waters of 'Big Mere.'

The Silhouetted Form of St Michael's Reflected in 'Big Mere'
Waiting around long after the sun had gone down, enabled me to capture this marvellous silhouette of St Michael's set against the clear evening twilight. A long exposure was required to capture the twilight and the crispness of the reflection indicates just how still the evening was.

Brightly Painted Canal Boats Outside Wrenbury Mill, South Cheshire
Whilst travelling through Wrenbury, these brightly painted canal boats caught my eye and I simply had to stop and photograph them. They had been repainted for the forthcoming boating season, and the brilliant red of their exteriors contrasted perfectly with the duller waters of the Shropshire Union Canal.

Misty Fields near Broxton
The warming glow of a Cheshire dawn adds atmosphere to morning mist as it forms in the fields around Broxton.
When conditions are right, scenes like this can often be seen in moist low-lying areas throughout the county.

Winter at Cholmondeley Castle
Cholmondeley Castle is home to one of the oldest families in Cheshire. Set upon the crest of a hill,
this fairytale castle enjoys an uninterrupted view over its 800-acres of parkland. Impeccable formal gardens,
sweeping lawns and landscaped lakes are set amongst stunning examples of Great British trees,
producing a magical setting for this wonderful stately home.

**Summer Water Cascade
in the Gardens of
Cholmondeley Castle**
This delightful little waterfall
tumbles gracefully down
through the castle gardens
and into Temple Garden Lake.
The ethereal movement of
the water has been achieved
by using a shutter speed of
several seconds.

The Cheshire Plain from Bickerton Hill
On a clear day the views from Bickerton Hill are astounding. The village in the foreground is
Brown Knoll with the wooded escarpment of Harthill rising beyond the village. Stanlow Oil
Refinery is just discernable as a tiny strip on the horizon, immediately right of the Silver Birch tree.

The Peckforton Hills in Winter, near Gallantry Bank
The Peckforton Hills extend from Peckforton Castle in the north to Gallantry Bank in the
south and are part of the mid-Cheshire Sandstone ridgeline that divides the Cheshire Plain.
In this image, early morning light casts low shadows over the snowy landscape.

Sunset over Peckforton Castle
The silhouetted battlements of Peckforton Castle rise above Peckforton Hills, providing the centrepiece for a glorious sunset. The ethereal movement in the clouds was achieved by using a long shutter speed and remarkably the colourful sky has not been enhanced in any way.

Peckforton Castle in Summer from the Battlements
Grade 1 Listed Peckforton Castle was built between 1844 and 1851 as a residence
for the slightly eccentric landowner and South Cheshire MP Lord John Tollemache.
Based on a Norman design, this magnificent fortress is today architecturally
recognised as a remarkable representation of a medieval castle.

An Idyllic Peckforton Estate Cottage in Spring
This stunning black and white cottage is typical of the dwellings to be found within the
Peckforton Estate and characterises the 'Magpie' buildings associated with Cheshire.
Tall chimneystacks and diamond-patterned windows evoke an atmosphere of days gone by.

Diamond-Patterned Window on Smithy Cottage, Beeston
Close up of a diamond-patterned window, this time a feature of picturesque
Smithy Cottage in the nearby village of Beeston. During the early days of glazing,
it was only possible to manufacture small pieces of glass, so fitting them into
diamond frames was both stylish and cost effective.

Golden Field of Wheat below Beeston Castle
Thirteenth-century Beeston Castle is one of the county's true landmarks. Standing 500 feet above
the Cheshire Plain upon its own outcrop in the mid-Cheshire sandstone ridgeline, it dominates
central Cheshire's skyline. This view is from the north and one can also see the battlements
of Peckforton Castle rising above the farmhouse in the middle distance.

Red Poppies below Beeston Castle
Another view of Beeston Castle, this time taken from the south.
It shows the characteristic triangular mound that the castle sits upon.
In this image bright red Poppies vie for attention amongst a field of ripening crops.

Harvesting in the Shadow of Beeston Castle
A quintessential English summer scene is played out here below Beeston Castle where a tractor collects the silage being harvested by a forage harvester. In this image, glimpses of the extensive ramparts of Beeston Castle can be seen winding their way around the wooded escarpment.

Sunset over the Shropshire Union Canal, near Beeston
This sunset was captured on a winter's evening from the bridge near Wharton's Lock just north of
Beeston Castle. The hazy orb of a winter sun has been captured moments before it enters a cloudbank
looming on the horizon and both are perfectly reflected in the still waters of the canal.

Springtime at 'Bunbury Cottage', Bunbury
Bunbury nestles amongst rolling farmland and quiet leafy lanes, 2 miles east of the
Peckforton Hills in central Cheshire. The village is famed for its abundance of black and white
timber-framed houses, which are a delightful feature of this charming little commuter village.

Fog-filled River Gowy Valley at Sunrise, near Bunbury
In this image, cool morning air flows down the hillside, condensing on contact
with the warming waters of the River Gowy, thus creating a rolling
blanket of mist and fog illuminated by a perfect Cheshire sunrise.

'Tudor Cottage' in Spring, Tattenhall
A perfect Cheshire scene is played out here in the historic village of Tattenhall
where a selection of colourful spring flowers frames the medieval black and white,
somewhat aptly named, 'Tudor Cottage' on Church Bank.

Cheshire Blue Lavender, Duddon, near Tarporley
This is a scene more reminiscent of Provence in France, rather than the heart of Cheshire.
Cheshire Blue Lavender is a small cottage industry boasting half an acre of different varieties of
this beautiful scented plant. Here, visitors can wander at will through the neat purple rows of
Lavender, selecting their own crop in surely one of the most tranquil settings in the county.

The Swan Inn and Tarporley High Street, Tarporley
Tarporley is an affluent mid-Cheshire commuter village with a plethora of interesting buildings. The Swan Inn
dating from 1769 was originally an old coaching inn and is one of the village's oldest and best-known buildings.
It is home to the Tarporley Hunt, the oldest hunt in England, who hold their meetings in the famous 'Hunt Room.'

Stocksbank and Lilac Cottages, Tiverton, near Tarporley
Most visitors to Cheshire will never have heard of Tiverton, even though many will have driven
through it. This charming village sits to one side of the busy A49 trunk road just south of Tarporley.
These traditional 'Cheshire Brick' cottages can be found bordering the village green.

Close up of the 'Church House', Tarvin
Tarvin's most famous building nestles in the shadow of St Andrew's Church
on the main village road. The timber framed 'Church House' dates from 1565
and its exquisite exterior displays a similar pattern to that of Cheshire's most
famous manor house, Little Moreton Hall near Congleton.

Church Street, Tarvin
Tarvin village is a curious mix of Medieval, Georgian and modern architecture that nestle together along both sides of the main road. In this image we see the black and white sixteenth-century 'Church House' put into context with examples of the aforementioned buildings.

Sunrise at Blakemere Moss, Delamere Forest

Blakemere Moss is a large low-lying area of Delamere Forest, which has recently been flooded by the Forestry Commission to provide a nature reserve and Site of Special Scientific Interest (SSSI). Captured here at first light, the early morning mist dances above the water's surface, whilst the first rays of sunlight illuminate radio masts on Eddisbury Hill.

Cyclists in Delamere Forest
Over half a million people visit Delamere Forest each year, drawn to discover the delights
of Cheshire's largest woodland. Easy parking, safe way-marked trails and an abundance
of wildlife all combine to make the Forest an ideal day out for all the family.

Ancient Beech Tree in the Heart of Delamere Forest
Modern day Delamere Forest grosses just 1300 acres of mature Oak, Beech and Coniferous trees.
This is in stark contrast to medieval times, when the Norman Earls of Chester enjoyed hunting
rights over a massive forested area stretching from Nantwich in the south up to the Mersey Estuary.

**First Rays of Morning Light
Illuminate the Spring
Canopy of Delamere Forest**
Originally called the Forest of
Mondrum and Mara, the
Norman kings changed it to
'Forest de la Mare' – literally
'the forest of the lake.'
Out of this, the name of
Delamere has evolved.

Hatchmere at Sunset, near Delamere Forest
Hatchmere is another Site of Special Scientific Interest (SSSI), this time located on the eastern fringe of Delamere Forest, beside the B5152 road to Frodsham. The sun's orb has been captured moments before it sinks slowly below the distant trees of Delamere Forest.

Stanlow Oil Refinery at Night

When travelling the M56 motorway in the vicinity of Chester, one cannot help but notice the giant Stanlow Oil Refinery. How can beauty be found in such a place? The answer can be found after dark, when the twinkling lights from a multitude of bulbs illuminate the Cheshire sky in a visual display normally seen only in large cities.

**Wild Flower Meadow
in Summer, near Alvanley**
The UK's Woodland Trust
has created a special new
wood in Cheshire close to
Alvanley. Wheeldon Copse
was planted with wild flowers
as part of an innovative and
successful experiment in
the suppression of invasive
weeds. In addition to giving
the saplings a head start, an
offshoot of the project was
the stunning riot of summer
colour we see here.

The Mersey Estuary from Frodsham Hill
This panoramic view looks out from 'Mersey View' on Beacon Hill. Beyond the town is the M56 motorway, and then Frodsham Marshes extend to the River Weaver. The Weaver flows right to left past the chemical works, joining the Manchester Ship Canal on the far left side, with the Mersey Estuary behind.

Hale Lighthouse and the River Mersey at Dawn, near Widnes
Hale lighthouse is Cheshire's only lighthouse. It stands 2 miles downstream from the Runcorn
Transporter Bridge on the northern bank of the River Mersey, close to the border with Merseyside.
Decommissioned in 1958, it now forms part of a private residence.

The Runcorn and Widnes Transporter Bridge at Night
Opened in 1961, the Runcorn/Widnes Transporter Bridge carries traffic nearly 200 feet above the
River Mersey. Its elegant arch and tangled mass of steel girders are brilliantly floodlit during
the hours of darkness, offering a dramatic addition to the Cheshire skyline.

Chemical Works and River Mersey at Sunrise, near Runcorn
Man's unfortunate influence upon the landscape of the Mersey Estuary is difficult to ignore, as is the pollution he has inflicted upon it. This though is quietly changing as the Environment Agency enforce greater controls for the good of our planet. Here, the bright lights of an industrial chemical works are reflected in the River Mersey pre-dawn glow.

Rock Savage Refinery and the River Weaver at Night, near Runcorn
Another industrial giant on the banks of the River Mersey, this time the large oil and gas refinery
attached to Rock Savage Power Station is reflected in the River Weaver. The blurring of the reflected
lights is due to movement in the flowing water over a long time exposure.

Fiddler's Ferry Power Station near Widnes
Two further landmark buildings from northern Cheshire are featured on these pages. This image shows the giant
cooling towers of Fiddler's Ferry Power Station belching out its vapour by-products into a clear blue sky.
This 2000 mega-watt power station is sited alongside the River Mersey from where it takes its water requirements.

The Nuclear Research Laboratory in Spring, Daresbury
The second landmark in this area is mushroom-shaped Daresbury Nuclear Research
Laboratory, photographed here above a vibrant yellow field of rapeseed. After years of a
decline in its fortunes, the laboratory has again recently moved to the forefront of
pioneering technology as a national centre for accelerator science.

The Golden Gates of Warrington Town Hall
The undeniable jewel in Warrington's crown is the golden gates of its Town Hall. These magnificent gilded, cast iron gates were made at Ironbridge in Shropshire and originally meant for erection outside the Prince of Wales' Sandringham Estate. They were instead purchased for the town in 1895.

Traditional Narrowboat and Bridgewater House at Lymm
A tranquil scene in the large Cheshire village of Lymm sees the whitewashed walls of
Bridgewater House beautifully reflected in the Bridgewater Canal. Lymm is a popular
stopping-off point for a multitude of pleasure-boaters that use the canal for leisure.

Traffic Trails on the Busy M56 Link to the M6 near Lymm
Motorways are often perceived as scars on the landscape, but when time and conditions
are right, they can be photographed in a most appealing manner. In this image, a long
time exposure makes the rush hour traffic on the M56 motorway record as colourful trails
of light, whilst on the horizon the final moments of twilight light up the night sky.

Gathering Storm near Higher Whitley

Conditions on the edge of a storm can be fantastic for landscape photographers. Clarity of light combined with brooding cloud masses can inject atmosphere into an image. Here, late evening sunlight illuminates the stormy base of a Cumulonimbus cloud, providing a perfect setting for a field of hay bales.

Arley Hall in Spring
Rowland Egerton-Warburton built Arley Hall in the Victorian-Jacobean style to the design of
Nantwich architect George Latham. This magnificent building along with the substantial gardens
and parkland have been owned and maintained by the same family for over 500 years making
it one of the few remaining landed estates in Cheshire in its original ownership.

Bluebell Glade in Big Wood, Arley Hall Estate
The Arley Estate has been offering springtime bluebell walks deep
into the heart of its 100-acre 'Big Wood' for many years now.
Volunteer guides lead visitors into the numerous bluebell glades,
offering a magnificent view of these British wild flowers.

Autumn Colours in Great Budworth
A stunning display of autumnal colours complements the delightful whitewashed
cottages on School Lane. Great Budworth is perhaps Cheshire's most attractive
village and has been described as 'a rare bit of Tudor England.'

Fishing Boats on Iced-up Budworth Mere
This wintry scene was captured during one of Cheshire's coldest winters. It was so cold in fact that Budworth Mere actually froze over. A deep coating of icy hoar frost clings to the trees on the far bank reinforcing the image of freezing conditions.

Children Playing in a Bluebell Glade, near Little Leigh
In a scene typical of many Cheshire woods in late spring, two young children enjoy the
visual splendour and distinctive aroma of a bluebell wood. Bluebells appear only for a few
short weeks after daffodils begin to wane and before trees develop their full canopy.
Increasingly though, the magical sight of a bluebell glade seems a difficult landscape to discover.

**First Light in Fryers
Rough Wood,
near Little Leigh**
The first rays of morning
sunlight filter through
the canopy of
Fryers Rough Wood.
The wood is privately
owned, and this enables
the bluebells to thrive
without man's interference.

Black and White Acton Bridge Spanning the River Weaver
Acton Bridge carries traffic on the busy A49 trunk road over the River Weaver.
It was built by Joseph Parks & Sons Ltd of Northwich and was officially opened to traffic
on 27th November 1933. With a span of 250 feet and weighing 800tons, it was the first bridge
to rest on a floating pontoon in the country and was a marvel of engineering at that time.

Early Morning Fog on the River Weaver, near Acton Bridge
The first rays of sunlight penetrate early morning fog to illuminate an old tugboat moored on the
southern bank of the River Weaver. The boat was built in 1949 by Pimblotts Boatyard in Northwich for
work on the Manchester Ship Canal and operated between the Bridgewater Canal and Manchester Docks.
It has now been purchased locally for renovation and will once more become 'Queen of the River.'

Narrowboat on the Trent and Mersey Canal, near Acton Bridge
In this classic late summer landscape, a beautifully painted narrowboat lies moored
on the banks of the Trent and Mersey Canal, whilst beyond the hawthorn hedge,
harvested hay bales sit drying in the sunshine.

Spectacular Sunrise with Silhouetted Trees near Little Leigh
This image shows what nature is capable of in the pre-dawn light before sunrise cuts the horizon.
Still below that horizon, the sun sends out light to illuminate the clouds far above the silhouetted trees
and fields we see here. A small finger of cloud is lit up with a fiery glow and one could be forgiven for
thinking that this may be the 'Finger of God' singling out his favourite tree for all to see.

Detail of Old Salt Truck, The Lion Salt Works, Marston
The 'Lion Salt Works' is the UK's last surviving open pan salt works and
was recently upgraded from Grade 2 status to that of Scheduled Ancient
Monument. Desperately in need of restoration, at the time of writing it
has just secured a £5 million grant from the Heritage Lottery Fund.
The extraordinary colour, texture and detail of this abandoned railway
salt truck was simply crying out to be photographed.

Sunset over Marston Flash, near Northwich
Driving home from the Lion Salt Works took me past Marston Flash as the sun was beginning to set.
The clouds above me looked interesting, so I decided to stay for a little while. Ten minutes later I
was lucky enough to see this marvellous sunset. Sometimes luck plays a big part in photography.

The Fully Restored Anderton Boatlift, near Northwich
Nicknamed 'the cathedral of the canals,' the Anderton Boat Lift was built in 1875 to link
the River Weaver with the Trent and Mersey Canal over a height of 50 feet. Having lain
derelict for many years, this Victorian marvel of engineering has now been restored to full working
order and was re-opened in March 2002. Today, it is one of Cheshire's main tourist attractions.

Evening Light on St Wilfrid's Church, Davenham
St Wilfrid's parish church towers over the surrounding landscape at the end of a clear winter's day.
The current church spire dates from 1680 and has been struck twice by lightning, firstly in 1850 and
again a hundred and thirty years later. Late evening sunlight has revealed the subtle hollows in the
foreground field, whilst the church spire's clock glows radiantly in the final moments of daylight.

Waterside Apartments Reflected in the River Weaver, Northwich
The town of Northwich is undergoing a radical change. Under the 'Northwich Vision' project, this former
salt town is to undergo a complete metamorphosis of the River Weaver area at a cost of over £200 million.
Here, the first phase in the development sees the site of an old council depot and desolate unpaved
car park, converted into magnificent waterside homes.

Apartment Reflections in the River Weaver, Northwich
A little while after the previous image was taken, a slight breeze disturbed
the still morning. The resulting ripples created by this wind produced a
beautiful abstract vision of the apartments on the surface of the River Weaver.

Fireworks Display at Verdin Park, Northwich
Northwich's Verdin Park has hosted the annual November 5th celebrations for over thirty years and is one
event not to miss in the town's calendar. Staged purely for charity, this professional firework display has been run
safely and efficiently by a partnership between the Northwich Rotary Club and Roundtable for many years.

Traffic Trails Over Town Bridge, The Bullring, Northwich
Town Bridge is one of two swing bridges that span the River Weaver in the town centre.
It was built in 1899 and was required to rest on a floating pontoon because of subsidence
associated with Northwich's extensive salt mining. Together with Hayhurst Bridge a
little upstream, they are the oldest electric swing bridges in the world.

Lone Tree at Sunset, near Sandiway
Late one evening, the shape of this solitary silhouetted tree caught my interest against the setting sun.
Rapidly cooling air was condensing in the fields all around me forming pockets of mist, and I
knew instinctively there was a photograph to be taken. The result shows that even a bare tree can
form the centrepiece for an interesting image, when nature works her magic on the landscape.

Rainbow over Petty Pool Wood, near Sandiway
The colourful arc of a rainbow brightens the sky over Petty Pool Wood near Sandiway. The intensity of a dark, brooding
rain cloud ensures that the colours of this particular rainbow are vividly portrayed over an early spring landscape.

St Mary's Church Spire and the Village of Whitegate
Evening sunlight casts long shadows over the landscape surrounding Whitegate village,
beautifully illuminating its early autumn colours. Set in the centre of modern-day Cheshire,
Whitegate is a charming village made famous as the location for thirteenth-century Vale
Royal Abbey financed by Edward I.

'New Pool' in Autumn, Whitegate
'New Pool' is a haven of tranquillity, known to few outside the village boundary.
In this image, the marvellous autumn colours in the distance are complemented by dappled sunlight sneaking
through the surrounding trees and illuminating the near bank. A finer autumnal setting is hard to imagine.

Early Morning Mist Hovers above the Weaver Navigation, near Winsford
As delicate hues of early morning light paint the sky, air in contact with the Weaver Navigation condenses, creating a blanket of swirling mist that spills over onto the surrounding riverbanks. The Weaver Navigation enabled cheap Lancashire coal to be transported to the saltpans of Winsford, and the resulting salt products back for export from the county.

Christmas Lights Adorn a Private House in Winsford
The tradition of decorating one's house in a multitude of Christmas lights seems to be
gaining in popularity, with sometimes whole streets competing against one another.
The owner of this house has been observing the tradition for over ten years and says
his inspiration is the look of delight on small children's faces when passing by.

Saxon Crosses in the Market Place, Sandbach
One of Cheshire's wonders, these superbly decorated eighth or ninth century Saxon Crosses stand in the
Market Place at Sandbach and are amongst the finest examples to be found anywhere in the country.
The taller of the two crosses is over 16 feet high and the smaller is about 11 feet high.

Sunrise over Sandbach Heath Church, near Sandbach
The church of St John the Evangelist was built in1861 to the designs of eminent
architect George Gilbert Scott. Gothic in style, the walls are constructed of local
stone quarried from Mow Cop and the roof is of Westmorland green slates.

St Mary's Parish Church in Springtime, Nantwich
Known locally as 'the cathedral of south Cheshire,' fourteenth-century St Mary's church is one of the finest medieval churches in the country. Constructed of local red Cheshire sandstone, it is an amazing centrepiece for a town offering so much historic interest that it would be impossible to even scratch the surface of it here.

Sweet Briar Hall on Hospital Street, Nantwich
One of Nantwich's oldest and most beautiful structures, Sweet Briar Hall was built in 1450 and
was one of very few buildings to survive the Great Fire of 1583 that devastated most of the town.
It is a striking example of a Cheshire black and white half-timbered 'magpie' building.

St Chad's Tower, Wybunbury, near Nantwich
Built in the fifteenth century, solitary Wybunbury tower is one of Cheshire's curiosities.
Originally part of a church, the medieval builders made a big mistake when choosing a
site for it. Springs below the foundations led to subsidence, and despite rebuilding the
church five times, it was eventually demolished, leaving this solitary sandstone tower
which actually leans approximately two feet out of true.

Church of St James the Great and 'The Shambles,' Audlem
Seen here dressed for its annual carnival, Audlem is one of Cheshire's most southerly villages and dominated by the huge thirteenth-century sandstone church of St James the Great. The structure supported by eight Tuscan pillars is 'The Shambles' and was the old market hall where bear baiting took place right up until the mid nineteenth century.

Mow Cop Castle and the Cheshire Plain, Cheshire / Staffordshire Border
The landmark structure of Mow Cop Castle stands over 1000 feet above sea level
straddling the border between Cheshire and neighbouring Staffordshire.
It was constructed as a summerhouse in 1754 by the Baker-Wilbraham family
of nearby Rode Hall, and was one of the very first English follies ever to be built.

Twilight at Mow Cop Castle, Cheshire / Staffordshire Border
This image of Mow Cop Castle was taken long after all other visitors had departed. The purple sky is created by the final seconds of twilight on a clear autumnal night. Moments later, the castle and hillside descended into inky blackness.

Little Moreton Hall in Winter, near Congleton
The single feature that has come to symbolise the county of Cheshire is its abundance of half-timbered black and white so-called 'magpie' buildings. Above all others, the fifteenth-century moated Elizabethan manor house of Little Moreton Hall is surely the finest example in all England, let alone Cheshire. This image shows the fantastic light available to the photographer on a cold, clear winter's day.

Frozen Moat at Little Moreton Hall, near Congleton
This image was taken during another visit to the hall, where the temperature had been consistently below freezing over a period of days and had frozen the moat! Stunning winter light is again provided by Mother Nature, who has also turned the surrounding landscape into a snowy winter wonderland.

Daffodils on the Village Green, Astbury
Astbury is a quintessential Cheshire village complete with historic church, ancient houses
and half-timbered 'magpie' cottages all surrounding a triangular village green.
In springtime the green is covered with a wonderful display of daffodils.

Looking East from Bosley Cloud Towards the Peak District National Park
Towering over the Cheshire countryside to a height of 1125 feet (343m) is the distinctive landmark of
Bosley Cloud. 'The Cloud' as it is known locally, provides extensive views over the whole of Cheshire.
Here we look eastward towards Cheshire's own slice of the Peak District National Park.

Spring Lambs near Holmes Chapel
This image has the aaaah factor! These adorable lambs were investigating
the base of this tree trunk and were relatively oblivious to my attempts at
photographing them. The low rays of early morning sunlight provide the
necessary lighting required to bring out the texture of their fleeces.

Gawsworth Old Hall, Gawsworth
The stunning half-timbered manor house of Gawsworth Old Hall dates mainly from the mid fifteenth century and was home to Mary Fitton rumoured to be the 'Dark Lady' of Shakespeare's sonnets. During the summer months a large stage is erected on the lawns in front of the house, creating an atmospheric backdrop for musical extravaganzas and theatrical performances.

Jodrell Bank Radio Telescope, near Goostrey
The giant steel MK1A Radio Telescope of Jodrell Bank dominates the landscape of central Cheshire.
Completed in 1957, it weighs over 3200 tons and rises 250 feet over the surrounding countryside.
In this late summer scene, traditional hay bales are stacked in harvested fields, whilst the bright red
berries of a Rowan tree add a vibrant splash of colour to the landscape.

Jodrell Bank Radio Telescope at Sunrise, near Goostrey
I nearly turned back on the way to this location as the clouds seemed leaden and grey in the dim light of early morning – but sometimes one must persevere and expect disappointment. This however, was not the case here. Lasting only a few seconds, as the mist in the fields below Jodrell Bank begins to disperse, the sun fleetingly illuminates a mainly cloudy Cheshire morning. Seconds later the colours had vanished.

**The Church of St Peter and
St Paul in Winter, Marton,
near Congleton**
Reputed to be the oldest
timber-framed church in
Europe, Marton church
is shown here bathed in
brilliant winter sunlight.
The magnificent quality of
evening light reflecting off
a snowy landscape has
caused the glorious purple
hue present in both the
snow and clouds.

Sunset over Pylons at Monks Heath, near Alderley Edge
Another atmospheric image, this time of a relatively mundane object that would usually not
warrant a second look. The symmetrical silhouette of this pylon takes on an almost
abstract form, as a glorious sunset sets the evening Cheshire sky on fire.

Market Place and the Town Hall at Night, Macclesfield
The tail lights of a passing vehicle add a vibrant splash of colour to the
autumn twilight in this view of 'Market Place' in Macclesfield's town centre.
Francis Goodwin designed the town hall in 1823. The building is the
headquarters for Macclesfield Borough Council.

Evening Twilight in Prestbury Village, near Macclesfield
The village of Prestbury is one of the most attractive in Cheshire and is ideally situated for routes to and from
the Manchester conurbation.   How appropriate then, to capture this affluent little commuter village during the
twilight hour featuring traffic trails of weary commuters returning from a day in the city.

Spring at Henbury Hall, Near Macclesfield
Henbury Hall was designed by Julian Bicknell and follows Palladio's design for his
'Villa Capra.' One of only two Palladian villas built in recent years in this country the hall
was completed in 1987 and is set within 12 acres of beautifully landscaped gardens.
Occasionally the gardens are open to the public.

Nether Alderley Mill in Summer, near Alderley Edge
This charming fifteenth-century watermill is one of only four working corn mills in Cheshire.
Once abandoned and in a state of disrepair, under the custodianship of the National Trust its interior
and workings were fully restored in the 1960s. Inside, low beams with flooring connected by
wooden ladders are all encased within the original Elizabethan heavy oak framework.

Summer Cricket Match at Alderley Edge Cricket Club
The ornate façade of Alderley Edge Cricket Club forms a charismatic backdrop for this most
traditional of English sports. The cricket club was formed in 1870 and plays on land
bequeathed to it by the de Trafford family who were prominent landowners at the time.

Autumnal View from Stormy Point on 'The Edge,' Alderley Edge
'The Edge' is a 600-foot sandstone escarpment rising dramatically above the Cheshire Plain.
Although mainly wooded, within its 227 acres are significant gaps that provide outstanding
views over the countryside towards the Pennine hills and distant skyline of Manchester.
Stormy Point is one such gap and here we see a magnificent autumnal view from 'The Edge.'

Christmas Lights on King Street, Knutsford
Knutsford is a very attractive old market town with a plethora of interesting buildings to
discover. In this image, King Street is decorated for Christmas and the distinctive structure of
Gaskell Tower can be seen overshadowing a selection of the town's attractive old buildings.

Rhododendrons and Mansion House, Tatton Park, near Knutsford
Home to the Egerton family for over 400 years, today the 2000-acre estate of Tatton Park is one of the
National Trust's most popular attractions. The handsome Georgian Mansion House is the jewel in
Tatton's crown and is shown here in late spring, framed by a dazzling display of Rhododendrons.

Spider's Webs, near Rostherne
With landscape photography, sometimes it is rewarding to thoroughly investigate the area
around you instead of becoming distracted by the big picture. Such was the case here.
Whilst shooting the delights of Rostherne Mere early one morning, I noticed the light
brilliantly illuminating the intricate designs of these dew-covered spiders' webs.

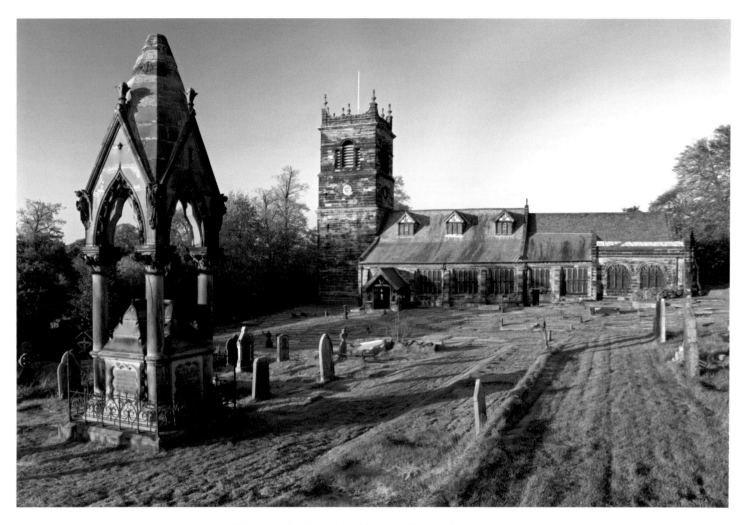

Evening Light on St Mary's Church, Rostherne
Evening sunlight casts a golden glow over the glorious sandstone monuments and exterior walls of
St Mary's church in Rostherne. A church has been in existence here since 1188 but most of the present
structure is eighteenth century. St Mary's was the original parish church for the Knutsford area.

Dunham Massey Hall, near Altrincham
Dunham Massey is a Georgian mansion with Edwardian additions. It was formerly the home
of the 10th and last Earl of Stamford, who bequeathed the estate to the National Trust in 1976.
The extensive formal gardens and parklands surrounding the house are exquisite and include
tree-lined avenues, tranquil ponds and its own deer park.

Passenger Connecting-corridor, Manchester International Airport
This futuristic image is of the automated walkways in a passenger-connecting corridor between terminals 1 and 2
at Manchester airport. The airport straddles the border between Cheshire and Greater Manchester.

School Children Maypole Dancing in the Village of Styal
Borne out of the Industrial Revolution, the village of Styal was developed and fashioned
by the factory pioneer Samuel Greg, who built houses here for his workers at nearby
Quarry Bank Cotton Mill in the late 1700s. Here we see children at the local primary
school practice for their annual village maypole dance.

Front Elevation of Adlington Hall, Adlington, near Macclesfield
Another of Cheshire's grand estates and home of the Legh family since 1315, Adlington Hall is situated within 2000 acres landscaped in the style of 'Capability Brown.' This is the Georgian south front of the Hall with a portico of six impressive stone pillars.

Lyme Park and its Lake Reflection, Lyme Park, near Disley
Country seat of the Legh family for over 600 years, Lyme Park is the largest and most impressive
mansion house in Cheshire. It will be familiar to many visitors as 'Pemberley' from the BBC's
adaptation of Jane Austen's novel *Pride and Prejudice*. Its Palladian appearance is courtesy of Italian
architect Giacomo Leoni who designed the portico looking out over manicured gardens and a lake.

Evening Light on 'The Cage,' Lyme Park, near Disley
'The Cage' is an eighteenth-century former hunting tower that stands alone upon windswept 'Cage Hill' to the north of Lyme Park. Captured here at the end of a winter's day, the final rays of evening sunlight illuminate the sandstone walls of this unusual structure.

Peak District National Park Entrance Sign near Macclesfield
An old millstone has been pressed into service as an entrance marker
to one of Cheshire's most beautiful areas. Welcome to Cheshire's slice
of the Peak District National Park.

Autumn Colours at Lamaload Reservoir
Lamaload Reservoir lies in a picturesque wooded valley populated by larch and pine trees to the north of the A537 Macclesfield to Buxton road. It was completed in 1964 and supplies the nearby town of Macclesfield with drinking water.

Old Blue Boar Farm, near Rainow
Bright red early autumn berries cling to the Gritstone exterior of Old Blue Boar Farm
by the side of the Rainow to Saltersford road. Picturesque hamlets like this are scattered
amongst the hills and valleys of Cheshire's Peak District.

An Explosion of Autumn Colours in the Village of Rainow
A former giant of the Industrial Revolution, today this peaceful little village enjoys an enviable
setting amongst rolling hills on the very edge of the Peak District. Locally-quarried buff-coloured
sandstone used in the construction of its buildings, perfectly complements the autumn colours.

The Jenkin Chapel at Saltersford, Cheshire's Peak District
Jenkin Chapel was built in 1733 and stands on one of the ancient packhorse 'Salter's Ways'
between Cheshire and Derbyshire. Various theories are given for its name, but the most popular
says that it was named after a fiery Welsh preacher that regularly attended this spot.

Cheshire Peak District Scenery Viewed from close to the Cat and Fiddle Inn
This tranquil scene portrays the isolated setting of Torgate Farm in the middle distance, nestling
on rolling hills below the peak of Shutlingsloe. The marsh grass in the foreground hides the
infant waters of 'Tor Brook' flowing from its catchment area on the slopes of Shining Tor.

Gradient Signpost near Buxtors Hill
It is not uncommon to see a gradient sign like this within Cheshire's slice of the Peak District National Park,
however it is unusual to discover one that enjoys such a marvellous setting. The tree-covered hillside is
Yarnshaw Hill and in the distance are the high moorlands around the Cat and Fiddle Inn.

Cloudburst Through Gathering Storm over Croker Hill, near Wincle
The Croker Hill telecommunications mast stands firm in the face of a gathering storm, with shafts of brilliant sunshine illuminating the landscape all around its imposing form. The mast sits on the route of the picturesque 35mile Gritstone Trail that begins in Disley, hugging the eastern border of Cheshire and finishing near Kidsgrove in neighbouring Staffordshire.

Tegg's Nose Trail Sign upon a Millstone Grit Boulder, Tegg's Nose
Early morning light illuminates a small sign marking the Tegg's Nose Trail.
Side lighting has brought out the texture in both the sign and the
small lichens attached to the boulder.

Tegg's Nose Reflected in Bottom's Reservoir, near Langley
The scree-clad slopes of Tegg's Nose tumble down towards the still blue waters of Bottom's Reservoir, where the vibrant hues of gold, brown and russet adorn the lower slopes in a spectacular display of Mother Nature's finest autumn colours.

Autumn at Trentabank Reservoir, Macclesfield Forest
Larch trees provide a magnificent autumnal display of colour on the northern shore of Trentabank Reservoir,
contrasting markedly with the evergreen conifers that surround the plantation and make up the majority
of Macclesfield Forest. A mirror-like reflection on the reservoir perfects this tranquil scene.

Macclesfield Forest Reflected in Tegg's Nose Reservoir, near Langley
Once a vast royal hunting forest established by the Norman Earls of Chester, today Macclesfield Forest is a working timber forest grossing approximately 1000 acres of mainly coniferous trees interspersed with open moorland. In this image early morning light illuminates the autumn trees, reflecting them in the still waters of Tegg's Nose Reservoir.

Ridgegate Reservoir and Macclesfield Forest
This atmospheric view shows the proximity of Macclesfield Forest to the tranquil waters of Ridgegate Reservoir. The early morning light casts long shadows across the summer landscape, illuminating every tuck and fold of the countryside.

A Winter's Day at Ridgegate Reservoir on the edge of Macclesfield Forest
Ridgegate Reservoir is one of four feeder reservoirs in this vicinity that supply a significant
proportion of eastern Cheshire's fresh water. In particular Ridgegate and neighbouring
Trentabank reservoirs provide the nearby town of Macclesfield with its drinking water.
The blueness of the scene helps to convey the very cold winter conditions.

Ice Crystals on Frozen Timber in Macclesfield Forest
The concentric rings and rough texture featured on the sawn timber contrasts
markedly here with perfect needle-like ice crystals created by Mother Nature herself.
Together, they create their own mini winter-wonderland.

Forest Chapel in Winter, Macclesfield Forest
Forest Chapel dates from 1834 and is located in the tiny hamlet of Macclesfield Forest. It is famous for the 'Rushbearing Ceremony' held each year on the first Sunday following the 12th August when the chapel is adorned with plaited reeds, flowers and freshly cut rushes. This image shows the harsh winter conditions often prevalent at the chapel in winter.

**Stone Plaque on the side of
the Cat and Fiddle Inn on the A537
Macclesfield to Buxton Road**
The Cat and Fiddle Inn is the second
highest public house in Great Britain.
At 1690ft above sea level, it stands
a mere 42 feet lower than its rival –
the Tan Hill Inn located in the
Yorkshire Dales.

The Isolated Cat and Fiddle Inn set within its Winter Moorland Setting
The Cat and Fiddle is shown here in splendid isolation, its tiny form dwarfed by the high moorland hills that it stands upon. It is of course this isolation that attracts a multitude of visitors every year to the inn, drawn by the fresh clean air and fabulous Peak District scenery. A hardy flock of sheep can be just seen grazing in the lower left corner.

The River Dane Tumbling out of Pannier's Pool, Three Shires Head
Three Shires Head is a magical location where the county borders of Cheshire,
Staffordshire and Derbyshire all unite. Here we see the infant waters of the
River Dane tumbling out of Pannier's Pool below an ancient packhorse bridge.

A Rambler Admires the View above Pannier's Pool, Three Shires Head
This fourteenth-century packhorse bridge lies on an old 'Salter's Route' between Cheshire and
Derbyshire. It has a perfect single-span stone arch and low sidewalls that allowed mules to
cross the bridge without having to remove their heavily laden 'panniers' (or baskets).

Bottom of the Oven Village below the bulk of Shining Tor, in Winter
More of a hamlet than a village, 'Bottom of the Oven' is a collection of buff-coloured sandstone buildings situated at the head of a valley containing Clough Brook. This isolated little community recoils below the dominant mass of Shining Tor rising imposingly behind. At 1834ft (559m) above sea level, Shining Tor is the highest point in Cheshire.

Dryknowle Farm and Whetstone Ridge in Winter, near Wildboarclough
Dryknowle Farm, seen here bathed in glorious winter sunlight, is surrounded by an attractive mix of coniferous and deciduous trees that cling to the side of Yarnshaw Hill. Above it capped in snow, towers the bleak form of Whetstone Ridge rising to over 1600 feet with the oddly named tributary of 'Correction Brook' scything down the hillside to the valley below.

Isolated Barn on the Trail to Shutlingsloe, near Wildboarclough
It was the fantastic sky that encouraged me to stop and photograph this isolated barn on
a footpath leading to Shutlingsloe. The shape of the clouds seemed to emulate the distant
horizon and the low raking beams of sunlight showed off the landscape at its very finest.

Dry Stone Wall Leading to Shutlingsloe in Autumn
The turn of autumn is a magical time in Cheshire's Peak District. Here, the dry-stone wall cuts through the marsh grass, taking us towards the tree line and on up to the summit of Shutlingsloe, known locally as 'Cheshire's Matterhorn.'

The Peak of Shutlingsloe Viewed from the Summit of Shining Tor
To conclude *Cheshire Moods* we take a look at perhaps my favourite view of the county, which displays the true
beauty of Cheshire's Peak District. Here we see the Gritstone 'Tors' of Shining Tor framing distant Shutlingsloe,
regarded as Cheshire's only true peak. To the right, Macclesfield Forest carpets the hillside with the
telecommunication mast on Croker Hill standing tall on the far right.